C. PANG

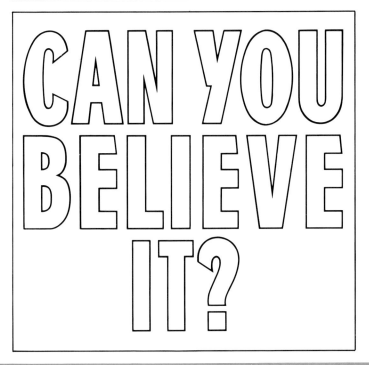

CAN YOU BELIEVE IT?

- THE NATURAL WORLD -

Written by
JENNY VAUGHAN

Illustrated by
SALLIE REASON

CHERRYTREE BOOKS

A Cherrytree Book

Designed and produced by Templar Publishing Company Limited,
Pippbrook Mill, London Road, Dorking, Surrey RH4 1JE

First published in 1990
by Cherrytree Press Ltd,
a subsidiary of
The Chivers Company Ltd,
Windsor Bridge Road,
Bath, Avon BA2 3AX

British Library Cataloguing in Publication Data
Vaughan, Jenny
  The natural world.
  1. Nature
  I. Title   II. Series
  500

  ISBN 0-7451-5078-0

Typeset by Southern Positives and Negatives (SPAN),
Lingfield, Surrey
Colour separations by Chris Willcock Reproductions,
Maidstone, Kent
Printed and bound by Proost N.V., Turnhout, Belgium

PICTURE CREDITS

Key: Top = t, bottom = b, left = l, right = r

All photographs supplied by Bruce Coleman Ltd.

Front cover: Erwin A. Bauer

Page 4 M. Timothy O'Keefe; page 9 Ken Balcomb; page 11 Dieter and Mary Plage; page 12 M. P. L. Fogden; page 14
Leonard Lee Rue III; page 15 Jane Burton; page 17 Steve Kaufman; page 18 J. Cancalosi; page 20 Erwin A. Bauer; page 24
Jeff Foott; page 25 Erwin A. Bauer; page 27 Gordon Langsbury; page 29 John Markham; page 31 Fritz Prenzel; page 33
Jane Burton; page 35 Steven Kaufman.

CONTENTS

? ? ? ? ? ? ? ?

1. Can fish shoot?

Yes, the archer fish shoots water at its prey. It lives in the mangrove swamps of the Far East and hunts insects. It swims through the roots of the mangrove trees looking for food above the level of the water. When it spots an insect on a leaf above, it squirts a jet of water at it. This jet can travel for up to a metre. If the insect is hit, it falls into the water and is seized by the fish.

2. Is the Great Barrier Reef really made of tiny skeletons?

*Coral reefs, such as Australia's Great Barrier Reef, are made by tiny sea creatures called **polyps**. When a polyp dies, it leaves behind a hard limestone skeleton. The skeletons left by millions of polyps living in a colony can make a reef that reaches 76 metres from the sea bottom.*

3. Is there an animal that throws its stomach at its enemies?

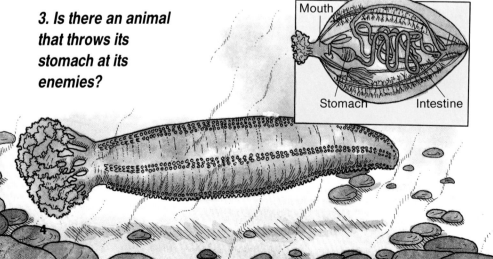

Mouth

Stomach   Intestine

Yes, some sea cucumbers can do this. Although they are named after a fruit, sea cucumbers are actually animals. There are several kinds. Some can throw all of their internal organs at an attacker. These cannot be drawn back into the body again; the animal has to grow a new set.

4

4. Do dragons exist?

It depends what we mean by 'dragons'. There are no fire-breathing, winged reptiles like those in story books, but a kind of lizard called a Komodo dragon does exist. It lives on a few small islands that form part of Indonesia. The Komodo is the biggest of all the lizards; it can grow to more than 3 metres long and weighs about 140 kilograms. It mostly eats the flesh of animals that have already died, but also hunts small deer, monkeys and other animals.

5. What would happen if greenflies had no enemies?

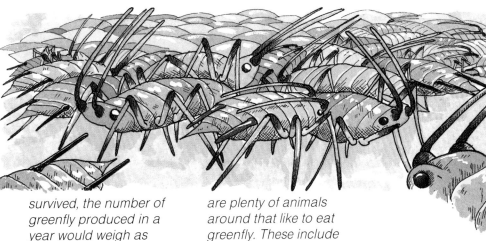

Female greenfly can give birth to young without having first mated with a male. One greenfly mother can have up to 25 young (all daughters) in just one day. Ten days later, these too can give birth. Someone once worked out that if they and all their descendants survived, the number of greenfly produced in a year would weigh as much as 500 million fat men! Luckily for us, there are plenty of animals around that like to eat greenfly. These include ladybirds and several kinds of birds.

7. Can a python swallow a goat?

A large python can be up to 10 metres long and can easily eat a small goat, just as it will eat gazelle, impala and other quite large mammals. There are even stories of a python eating a leopard. Usually, pythons prefer to eat smaller mammals, such as hares and rats. A python attacks its prey by springing out at it. Then it wraps its body around the animal and squeezes until the victim suffocates and dies. The python's jaws are hinged in such a way that they can dislocate in order to open very wide and so swallow objects bigger than themselves.

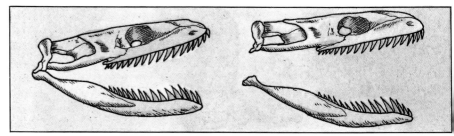

8. Do crocodiles cry?

Crocodiles have tear glands, just as we do, and often look as if they are crying. At times, they even make a sad howling noise. Because of this, people once believed that crocodiles were dishonest, pretending to cry and be sorry for the animal that they had just eaten.

6. Can you make soup from a bird's nest?

Yes, in China, soup made from birds' nests is a dish for special occasions. The nest used is made by a kind of swift. The swift eats small fish and other sea animals. It regurgitates these, mixes them with saliva and spits them out to make its nest. To make soup, the nest is boiled and then cooked with other ingredients. The nest itself does not taste of much – the flavour comes from the things cooked with it.

9. Do bats use 'radar' to find their way?

People often say that bats use 'radar' to find their way, but this is not strictly true. Radar works using radio waves, but bats find their way using **sonar** *– sound waves. In radar, the radio waves bounce back from solid objects and show up on a screen. Similarly, bats send out high-pitched sounds which bounce off solid objects, making an echo. The bat uses this echo to find its way in the dark and to locate insects which it eats.*

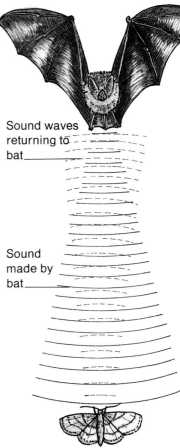

Sound waves returning to bat

Sound made by bat

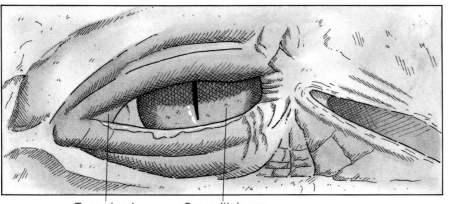

Tear gland   Crocodile's eye

10. Do some spiders carry their own air supply?

Water spiders live under water, catching and eating small creatures such as insect **larvae** (young). They need air to breathe while underwater and, to get it, each spider comes to the surface of the water and traps bubbles of air beneath its body. It then goes back under the water and releases the bubbles into its 'diving bell'. This is a balloon made from the spider's web and fixed between strands of water plants. The spider hides under this balloon, jumping out to catch its prey.

11. Are a butterfly's wings really covered in scales?

Butterflies and moths have delicate wings, often brightly coloured and with distinctive patterns. The colours and patterns are all formed by tiny scales on the upper surface of each of the four wings. They are easily brushed off if the butterfly is handled.

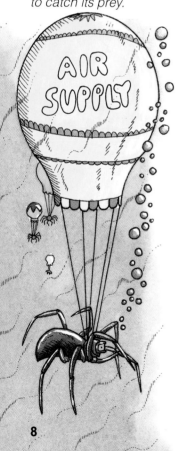

12. Do birds weave?

Weaver birds really do weave: that is how they get their name. These small birds are found in Africa and Asia. They live in large groups, many nesting together in one tree. The males build the nests, using palm fronds or grass stems. They start by weaving a few fronds into a loop and then go on to make a hollow ball. In doing so they may almost strip bare the tree on which they are living. Some kinds of weaver birds even weave a long entrance tunnel. When the nest is finished, the male attracts a female by hanging upside down underneath it. The female lays her eggs inside the nest, where they will be safe from predators.

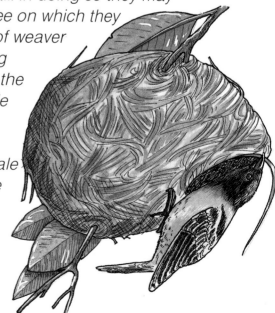

13. Can a chameleon really change colour?

Chameleons can change the colour of their skin from pale green to dark grey and many shades in between. They change to blend in with their background so they cannot be seen so easily by predators or their prey! This is called **camouflage**. They are not, however, the best colour-changers. A flatfish can almost match a chessboard if one is put underneath it.

14. How clever are dolphins?

Many scientists believe that dolphins are the most intelligent of all mammals – apart from humans. They have their own language, made up of whistles and clicks, which helps them to find their way in the open sea and to keep in contact with each other. In captivity, they are well known for their ability to learn tricks. There are many stories about wild dolphins helping stranded swimmers by giving them rides to safety. One dolphin, in New Zealand, used to guide ships through the Cook Strait, between the North and South Islands.

15. Can birds fly while they are asleep?

Yes, swifts sleep 'on the wing'. From radar pictures, we know that these birds sometimes spend the night gliding, thousands of metres up in the sky. It is thought that they sleep for short periods, carried along by air currents. They wake now and again to flap their wings.

16. Do hedgehogs snore?

Yes, they do. Hedgehogs sleep a lot. In summer, they curl up under a hedge and sleep from early morning until evening. They sometimes snore quite loudly at this time. At night, they hunt for insects, snails, slugs and worms. In winter, hedgehogs **hibernate**, *which means that they sleep very deeply and do not wake for months. During this time, they live on a store of fat that they have built up under their skin. Their body temperature drops and their heartbeat slows down – but they don't snore!*

18. Can a beetle hitch a ride on a bee?

Yes, the larvae of some kinds of blister beetles can do this. They hitch a ride from a solitary bee in order to get food. Each larva climbs on to a flower and waits for a bee to come along. When the bee lands, the larva fixes itself to the bee's body and is carried to its nest. There the larva waits for the bee to lay an egg. When the bee leaves the nest to collect food, the larva eats the egg.

17. Is it true that elephants never forget?

Elephants certainly have very good memories, as anyone who works with them will tell you. They can learn to obey many different kinds of signal – from a gentle kick behind the ears to an instruction given in words. Once an elephant has learned these signals, it does not forget them. Elephants also seem to remember people, whether they like them or not! They remember bad experiences, too, like getting a shock from an electric fence.

CAN YOU BELIEVE IT?

20. Can whales use bubbles to catch their food?

Humpbacked whales catch their food by making a 'net' of bubbles. These whales eat krill, shrimp-like animals that live in huge numbers in the Arctic and Antarctic seas. The whale catches a swarm of krill by swimming around it, under water, blowing bubbles as it moves. The krill are trapped inside the wall of bubbles and the whale can then swim upwards and eat them. Humpbacked whales are not the only ones to eat krill, though they are probably the only ones that catch it in this way. The blue whale, which is the largest mammal in the world, lives entirely on these tiny animals, which are only a few centimetres long.

19. What is a forest of stone?

*Trees, like other living things, can become **fossilized**. In Arizona, in the United States, there is a place known as the Petrified Forest, because of the many fossil logs found there. About 200 million years ago, when these fossils were living trees, they were engulfed by a flood. They stayed there covered by water, and gradually their tissues were replaced by minerals from the water. Eventually they hardened into rock.*

This photo shows the Kalahari Desert in Southern Africa after the rains have fallen.

12

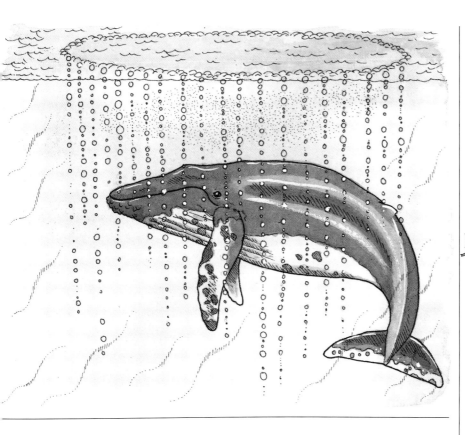

22. Can it rain frogs?

There are stories of frogs having fallen from the sky. Naturalists think that the tiny frogs must have been whipped up out of the water by strong winds and carried high into the sky. Later, when the winds dropped, the frogs 'rained' down, miles away.

23. Does a camel keep water in its hump?

No, but it can live for weeks without drinking. Camels' bodies are adapted to enable them to lose a lot of moisture without harmful effect. They get the moisture they need by eating desert plants. They do not store water anywhere in their bodies. The hump is a store of fat, which provides the camel with energy.

21. Can flowers grow in the desert?

Deserts often look bare and barren, but some flowering plants are specially adapted for life there. Short-lived plants survive the intense heat and low rainfall by being 'drought evaders'. Their seeds lie dormant in the sand until the rains come. Then the desert comes alive. The seeds germinate, flower and set seed all within a few weeks, and for a short time the desert is covered with a carpet of flowers. Other plants, cacti and succulents, for example, are 'drought resisters', storing water in their fleshy leaves or stems. Their flowers are usually large and colourful to attract insects for pollination, but they may bloom for only one day.

24. Can chimps use language?

Chimpanzees have different facial expressions for happiness, anger and for saying 'hello' to each other. They show that they are friendly by holding hands or embracing. They make many different kinds of noise, but naturalists do not think that they actually talk to each other using language in the way that humans do. Chimps that have been raised in captivity have learned to 'talk' to humans using the same sign-language as that used by people who cannot hear or speak. Some chimps have learned over a hundred words and can tell people what they want. Gorillas have also been taught how to talk to us in this way.

1. *This sign means 'dirty monkey'*
2. *This is the sign for 'bad'*

25. Do opossums really 'play possum'?

'Playing possum' means pretending to be dead. Instead of fighting or running away from an enemy, there are some animals that stay still and look dead. This seems to put off many predators which prefer to catch live food. The behaviour of the North American opossum gave rise to the expression 'playing possum'. If attacked, it goes limp, rolls over, shuts its eyes and lets its tongue hang out – enough to put off most of its enemies!

The Himalayan range of mountains is far inland and yet you can find fossilized sea shells there. These fossils were formed millions of years ago when the rocks that now form the Himalayas lay beneath shallow seas. Movements in the Earth's crust forced the land masses on either side of these rocks together, pushing the rocks upwards to form mountains.

26. Can a starfish grow new arms?

Yes, if a starfish is damaged and loses one arm, it can easily grow another. One group of starfish, Linckia, can even grow a completely new body from a piece of arm only a centimetre long.

27. How far can a bird fly?

No-one knows the longest distance ever flown by a bird. But we do know that some types of bird are capable of flying a very long way. Every year, for example, Arctic terns build their nests and rear their young in the northern polar region, the Arctic. At the end of the summer they set off for the southern polar region, the Antarctic, which is about 20,000 kilometres away. They spend the summer there, and then fly all the way back again.

Arctic

Antarctic

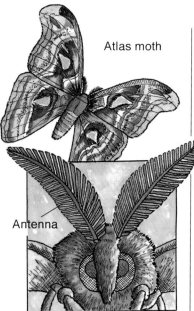

Atlas moth

Antenna

30. Do some animals really pretend to be other animals?

Many animals have evolved in such a way that they look like other, more dangerous animals. This helps to make them safe from their enemies. For example, the viceroy butterfly is harmless, but it looks like the poisonous monarch butterfly. Insect-eating animals leave the viceroy alone, mistaking it for its poisonous relative. In the same way, the kingsnake is harmless, but looks like the poisonous coral snake. If you look carefully, however, you can see that the order of the coloured stripes is different on each snake.

29. Can a moth smell its mate from a mile away?

Yes, some female moths produce a scent to attract male moths. The males can pick up this scent from 11 kilometres away. The male atlas moth is especially good at this. It picks up the scent with its very large, feathery antennae.

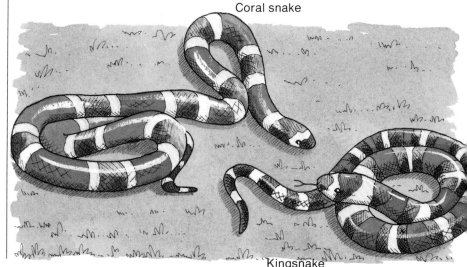

Coral snake

Kingsnake

31. How big is a 'giant' squid?

Squid are related to cuttlefish and octopuses. The largest squids belong to the group Architeuthis. In 1888 a specimen measuring a massive 17 metres was found in the seas around New Zealand. These huge creatures may well be the monsters described in early seafaring stories.

33. Can a frog have a 'frog' in its throat?

Yes, the male Darwin's frog hatches its young in the vocal sac in its throat. The female lays her frog-spawn (eggs surrounded by jelly) on the ground. The male watches over the spawn until it sees movements within the jelly. The movements mean that the eggs are about to turn into tadpoles. To keep them safe, the male takes them into his mouth. When the tadpoles have grown into tiny frogs, the male opens his mouth and out they jump!

32. Is there really a tree that is over 4,000 years old?

There is a tree in California called 'Old Methuselah', and it is over 4,000 years old. It is a Great Basin bristlecone pine like the one shown above. Some of these trees grow up to 21 metres high. They live for longer than any other tree – longer even than their relatives, the Rocky Mountain bristlecone pines, which live for 'only' 2,000 years.

34. Are electric eels actually electric?

Yes, but they are not really eels. The animals known as electric eels actually belong to a different family of fish. They are, however, long and thin, like real eels. They live in the rivers of the Amazon basin in South America and can give out an electric shock powerful enough to kill a horse. Their usual diet, however, consists of other fish and frogs.

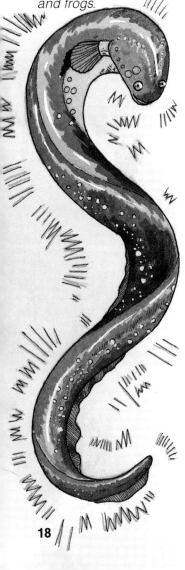

35. How big was the first horse?

The first horse was smaller than a dog. Called Eohippus or 'dawn horse', it was the ancestor of all horses living today. It was rather like a deer, with four long, splayed toes on each foot. It lived in forests. As the world's climate became drier, horses slowly developed longer legs for running over grassy plains. They also grew much larger and had only three toes on each foot. The outer toes gradually became smaller until, at last, there was only one toe, a hoof, on each foot.

Eohippus   Retriever

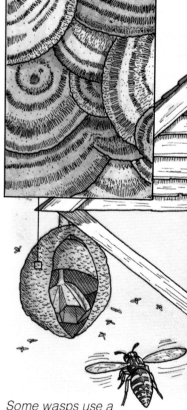

36. Where can you see a unicorn's horn?

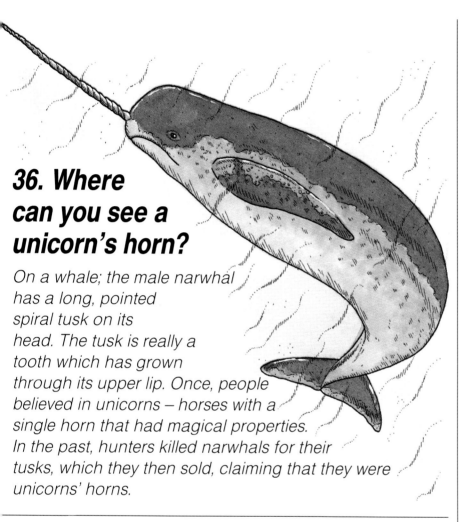

On a whale; the male narwhal has a long, pointed spiral tusk on its head. The tusk is really a tooth which has grown through its upper lip. Once, people believed in unicorns – horses with a single horn that had magical properties. In the past, hunters killed narwhals for their tusks, which they then sold, claiming that they were unicorns' horns.

Some wasps use a substance very like paper to make their nests. The queen wasp begins the nest in the spring. Using her mandibles (mouthparts) she scrapes wood fibres from a dead tree or post. She mixes these with saliva to form a little pellet of paste, which, when dry, is very like paper. With this, the queen builds a cluster of cells and into them lays her first eggs. These hatch into worker wasps, which look after the rest of her eggs, feed the young and continue the building of the nest.

37. Do dinosaurs still exist?

As far as we know, there are no dinosaurs alive today. The nearest living relatives are crocodiles and alligators – who belong to the same group of reptiles as the dinosaurs.

*The tuatara lizard from New Zealand (shown here) belongs to a group of reptiles called the **beak-heads** that existed even before the dinosaurs. It is the only one of this group left and it is known as a 'living fossil'. Some people think that a few dinosaurs may still be living. The famous Loch Ness monster may be one of these!*

Spiny anteater

39. Do any mammals lay eggs?

Most mammals give birth to live young. There are only two kinds that lay eggs. These are the spiny anteater (or echidna) and the duck-billed platypus. Both are found in Australia.

The platypus is a water animal. It makes a nest in a hole in a river bank and lays two eggs. These hatch after about 12 days and the young live on milk from their mother's body.

The spiny anteater lays one or two eggs a year and keeps them in a pouch in her body until they hatch.

Duck-billed platypus

40. Are there lizards that wrestle?

Some monitor lizards have wrestling matches in the mating season. One male will try to push another to the ground. The first one to succeed is the winner and will mate with the female. Monitor lizards may be quite fierce and can grow very large (the two-banded monitors shown here may reach 3 metres in length). They can fight and injure other animals, such as dogs. Yet when the lizards wrestle with each other, they rarely get hurt.

41. Does a sloth spend all of its life upside-down?

Sloths live in trees in the forests of South America and spend almost their whole lives hanging upside-down, holding onto branches with their strong claws. They even give birth to their young upside-down. Their fur does not grow downwards from the back to the stomach, as with most mammals, but in the other direction. This means that rain water runs off it more easily.

42. Is a bath sponge an animal?

It can be. Modern sponges are often made of plastic, but in the past, they were always real sponges – the skeletons of a kind of sea animal. Sponges live in warm seas at depths of 188 metres. There are about 3,000 different kinds, but the ones used as bath sponges come from the Mediterranean. A living sponge is made up of thousands of little cells. These cells draw water into the body of the sponge which it then sieves for food. The water is then flushed out of the body along with the animal's waste products.

43. Do people eat eggs that are 1,000 years old?

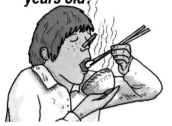

Yes, and no. In China, people eat what they call 'thousand-year-old eggs'. These are duck eggs, kept in lime, mud and ashes for about four months. This makes them look very ancient, hence their name. The whites turn brown and the yolks turn green!

44. Are cheetahs the fastest animals on Earth?

It is thought that cheetahs can run as fast as 100 kilometres an hour, but it is difficult to measure the exact speed of a wild animal. A cheetah only runs fast for short distances – in a long-distance race, a man would probably win. The cheetah uses its speed to catch gazelle and other wild animals of the African grasslands.

45. What is coal?

Coal is formed from ancient forests of tree ferns, giant horsetails and conifers. These grew in swamps, about 340 million years ago. When the plants died, they sank beneath the mud. Over millions of years, their remains were crushed and compacted by further layers of mud. Changes occurred in their chemical make up until eventually they turned to peat. Slowly the peat hardened and turned to coal. Fossilized remains of animals that lived in these ancient forests are often found in coal seams.

Plant remains fall into mud

Many layers build up and harden into coal

46. Can pigeons find their way home?

Yes, 'homing' or 'racing' pigeons are trained to fly home from places hundreds of kilometres away. No one knows exactly how they do it. They certainly use sight to help them, but some people believe that they can sense the Earth's magnetic field and, from this, work out in which direction they are flying.

47. Do cows have four stomachs?

*People sometimes say they have – but there is really only one, divided into four parts. These are the rumen, the reticulum, the omasum and the abomasum. When the cow swallows grass, it goes first to the rumen, where it is softened. Later on, this softened grass (or cud) is returned to the cow's mouth. The cow chews it for some time, then swallows it again. The food passes through the other three parts of the stomach where it is digested. Animals with this sort of stomach are called **ruminants**.*

1. Rumen
2. Oesophagus leading to mouth
3. Reticulum
4. Omasum
5. Abomasum
6. Intestine
A. Path of food before chewing cud
B. Path of food after chewing cud

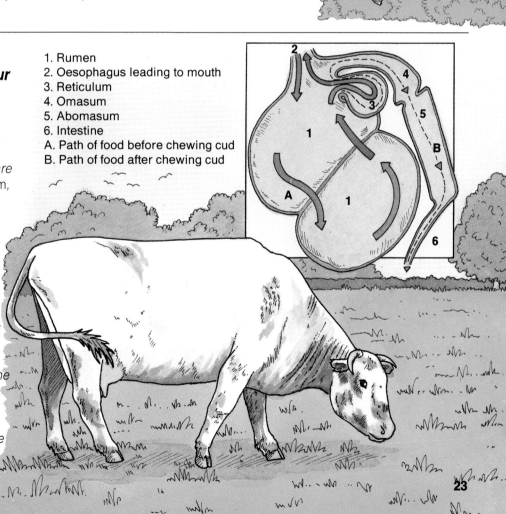

48. How long is a giraffe's tongue?

A giraffe's tongue can be as long as 40 centimetres. The animal uses it to grab leaves from the tips of branches. In the African savannah where it lives, there are few trees. Being tall, the giraffe is able to make the most of what trees there are. It can reach branches that other animals cannot.

49. Is a bald eagle really bald?

No, some birds, such as vultures, really are bald, but the bald eagle has plenty of feathers on its head and neck. It looks bald, from a distance, because these feathers are white. The bald eagle is the symbol of the United States of America and was once common. In the past, many of these eagles were shot and others have been harmed by pollution. Today, the bald eagle is a protected species. Large areas of its natural habitat are being preserved, and it is illegal to shoot them.

50. Do baboons tell lies?

Studies have shown that young baboons play all sorts of tricks on their parents, such as pretending to be hurt or afraid, so that they can get attention or extra food. This kind of play shows a high level of intelligence. In fact, baboons have been taught to do all sorts of things, including looking after a flock of goats.

51. Is it true that cats are never any wider than their whiskers?

Many people believe that a cat's whiskers are exactly the width of its body and that it uses them to check if it can get through a narrow space. Whiskers do help the cat feel its way in the dark – but lots of fat cats are wider than their whiskers!

52. Do centipedes really have 100 legs?

Yes, and some have even more! Certain types of centipede have as many as 177 pairs of legs, while others have only 15. Centipedes eat insects, spiders and worms. They kill their prey with a poisonous bite, not from their jaws but from a specially adapted pair of legs.

53. Can animals change colour in winter?

Yes, in countries where snow falls every year some animals are brown in summer and white in winter. These include stoats, some hares and a bird called a ptarmigan. The white colour makes them hard to see against the background of snow. We call this **camouflage**.

Summer plumage

Winter plumage

54. Can you use a spider's web as a fishing net?

Some tropical spiders make webs more than 2 metres across, with very thick, strong silk. In parts of south-east Asia, people use these as fishing nets. The web is removed using a stick. The stick is bent into a loop and pulled through the web. It comes away whole and ready to use.

Fully-grown koala

Young koala, about seven months old

55. Is a baby koala really smaller than someone's little finger?

Like all young marsupials, baby koalas grow to maturity in a pouch on their mother's abdomen. The newborn koala is pink, hairless, about 19 millimetres long and 5.5 grams in weight. At birth it crawls along its mother's fur into her pouch and fixes itself to a teat. It stays there for 6 months.

56. Is it true that a robin will fight its own reflection?

Robins seem very friendly birds to us, but they are not at all nice to each other. Each robin has its own territory, and will defend it against invading robins. It will even attack a tuft of red feathers fixed to a twig, mistaking it for a rival robin. It will certainly fight its own reflection in a window or a mirror.

When a male robin is looking for a mate, he has a problem. A female robin looks just like him, so he may begin by fighting her instead of courting her. During the nesting season, the female does not fight back, and so the male soon realizes who she is and allows her to stay.

57. Are there mummies of cats?

Yes. The Ancient Egyptians preserved human bodies as mummies before they buried them. They did the same with cats. The Egyptians believed in an afterlife into which the mummified people (and cats) would pass.

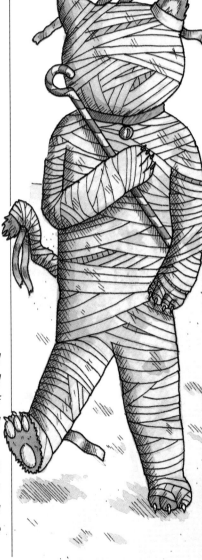

58. Can lizards run on water?

Yes, the basilisk lizard from Central and South America can run across water. It approaches the water very quickly on all four legs and runs across on two legs. The lizard is very light with long, widely spaced toes. This enables it to scuttle across the water's surface without sinking.

59. Are there really more than 1,000 kinds of flea?

Yes, and all of them live on animals' bodies and suck blood. The fleas we find most often are cat and dog fleas. Human fleas are rare now. In the past, fleas were sometimes kept as pets and made to do tricks in 'flea circuses'.

60. Do clothes moths actually eat clothes?

There are three different kinds of moth known as clothes moths. They all eat clothes, mainly those made of wool or fur. They prefer dirty clothes to clean ones. The moths themselves do not eat clothes; they lay their eggs on them. When the eggs hatch, the larvae eat the fabric, leaving tiny holes.

61. Is there a bird that has claws on its wings?

Hoatzins are birds from South America. They have claws on their wings when they hatch. The young birds use these to climb about in the trees. As they grow up, the claws disappear and the wing feathers grow. They are then able to fly.

29

62. Can animals sleep standing up?

Many animals sleep standing up. Birds usually sleep perched on a branch often with their head tucked under a wing. Many large mammals, such as elephants, usually sleep on their feet. This may be so that they can move quickly if danger threatens. It takes an elephant quite some time to get on to its feet again if it lies down. However, elephants do sometimes sleep lying down. They have been known to make a pillow of grass and branches to put their head on as they sleep.

63. Is there really an animal that has been around for 200 million years?

King crabs (which are also called horseshoe crabs) are almost exactly like a prehistoric animal that lived 200 million years ago. Fossils of these crabs can be seen in rocks in many parts of the world. They belong to a different group from other crabs and have no close relatives among animals living today. Scientists call them 'living fossils'. They are left-overs from millions of years ago.

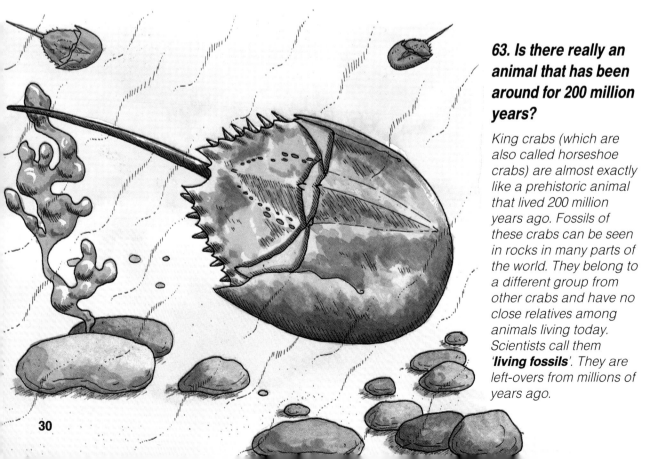

65. Do hummingbirds actually hum?

Yes, the humming sound comes from their wings which they beat back and forth so quickly that it enables them to hover above flowers to reach the nectar. Some hummingbirds beat their wings 80 times a second.

66. Could a spider eat a bird?

Huge spiders, up to 25 centimetres across, live in the forests of the Amazon basin. Instead of spinning webs to catch insects, these spiders chase and catch small mammals or take tiny hummingbirds from their nests.

64. Is it true that koalas never drink?

It is often said that koalas never drink, but this is not strictly true. A healthy koala gets all the moisture it needs from its main food – the tender shoots of eucalyptus trees. However, in dry places, or if the koala is unwell, it will seek out water to drink.

Koalas are very difficult to keep in captivity. They have been known to eat bread and milk, but they cannot live without their special diet of eucalyptus.

67. Do pondskaters really skate?

Pondskaters 'skate' on the surface of the water just as a skater does on ice. Pondskaters are insects with light bodies and long legs. They can slide on the water's surface because of 'surface tension' – a thin film that forms on the surface of the water. The pondskater's long legs spread the weight of its body out over a wide area. This prevents the insect from breaking the surface film and sinking.

68. How tall was the world's largest bird?

If you had lived between 25 and 65 million years ago, you would have had to watch out for Diatryma, the world's largest bird. It was over 3.5 metres tall and had a head as big as that of a small pony. Although it could not fly, it had very powerful legs for chasing its prey. It could probably run faster than other meat-eating animals, so it was not often beaten to a meal – or made into one!

69. Are moose antlers covered in velvet?

Moose are the largest of all deer. The male has antlers which it sheds in winter. New antlers start to grow in spring and, at first, the new antlers are covered with velvety skin. In late summer, when the antlers are fully grown, the velvet falls off.

70. Do goats make deserts?

Goats can turn poor land into desert, simply because they will eat almost anything. They will go to any lengths to reach plants and will strip the leaves and bark from trees, so that in the end the plants die. Without plant roots to hold moisture, the soil becomes dry and dusty and much of it blows away. The land then becomes desert.

71. Can plants grow on animals?

Yes, sloths never groom themselves and this allows tiny plants, called algae, to grow undisturbed on their coats. After a while, the sloths' fur becomes green with algae. This helps the sloths by making them hard to see among the green leaves of the rainforest where they live. Some kinds of moth lay their eggs in the sloths' fur. When the caterpillars hatch, they feed on the algae.

72. Do animals build towns?

Prairie dogs are a kind of North American ground squirrel. They live in large groups, and each individual digs its own burrow. A large number of burrows is called a 'town', and may cover up to 60,000 square kilometres. Prairie dogs have been so widely hunted that today's towns are becoming smaller and common only in national parks. When a town gets too crowded, some prairie dogs move off and start a new town on the edge of the old one.

73. Is it true that bees dance?

Honeybees can tell each other where to find food by 'dancing'. If a bee finds food, it goes back to the hive and makes a pattern of movements which looks like a dance. If food is nearby, it goes round in a circle. If food is further away, it dances in a circle crossed by a wiggly line. The number of wiggles and the direction of the dance tell other bees how far away the food is and in which direction.

74. Do Japanese monkeys take hot baths?

The weather in northern Japan can be very cold in winter, but the macaque monkeys that live there have a special way of keeping warm. They take long baths in the pools around hot volcanic springs, grooming each other and keeping warm. Of course, they have to come out now and again to look for food. They live on seeds and bark.

INDEX